ROYAL NAVY
IN FOCUS
IN WORLD WAR II

From the collection of Sydney Goodman
with captions by Ben Warlow

EDITOR'S NOTES

The photographs in this book have been selected from the archives of Sydney Goodman, who, like his father and his father before him, has been an avid collector of ship photographs. His grandfather and uncles served in the Navy, and their tales, together with his work in Devonport Dockyard, which brought him into close proximity with the ships themselves, fuelled his enthusiasm. He has developed a knowledge and passions for the vessels which is second to none. He now lives in retirement near Plymouth, so can devote many hours to his hobby He is fortunate in having a daughter who has an equal interest in these ships. It has been of great value to ship lovers generally that Sydney made such an effort to collect these photographs, which otherwise would have been lost to us, as many were destined for the waste bin. It is doubly fortunate in fact, as many were never available to the general public, and show ships as they were during World War II. He has given much of his time and energy in helping local newspapers, including the Dockyard publications, in making photographs from his collection available on suitable occasions so that interest can be engendered in the younger generation and happy memories brought to many older readers. This interest has been developed far and wide, and Sydney has made friends throughout the world who share his enthusiasm. Regrettably copy prints of these photographs cannot be provided - the task is simply too great.

The historical notes have been added by Ben Warlow, another Plymouth man, who served as an officer in the Royal Navy for over 37 years and who has a similar life-long interest in these ships. He too is retired concentrating on his lifetime's hobby!

M A CRITCHLEY
Liskeard
June 1994

ABERCROMBIE

The monitor ABERCROMBIE was one of two built during World War II, using the 15 inch guns originally mounted in the MARSHALL SOULT and MARSHALL NEY and other discarded monitors. ABERCROMBIE had her twin 4 inch guns mounted a deck higher than her sister, and her stern, as seen here, was reminiscent of an earlier era, with boats at davits. Completed in April 1943 on the Tyne, she bombarded during the Sicilian landings and at Salerno, being damaged by a mine in September 1943. After the war she became a turret drill ship at Chatham prior to being sold in December 1954.

ADAMANT

Built as a submarine depot ship by Harland and Wolff at Belfast, ADAMANT was completed in February 1942 and sent to the East Indies, but was diverted to Mombasa to act as a depot ship for escort vessels. In late 1942 she was despatched to Colombo to take up her proper duties, but was recalled again when the HECLA was lost. By mid 1943 she was at Trincomalee tending the 4th Submarine Flotilla and moved with them to Fremantle. Post War she was the Senior Officer's ship for the Reserve Fleet at Portsmouth from 1948-53 before taking care of the 3rd Submarine Squadron at Faslane until 1963. She then spent three years at Devonport with the 2nd Submarine Squadron before paying off. She arrived at Inverkeithing in September 1970 for breaking up.

ADVENTURE

The cruiser minelayer ADVENTURE was launched at Devonport Dockyard on 24 June 1924 being completed in December 1926. She was the only one of her type, and at the outbreak of war was busy laying mines in the Dover Strait, assisted by the small minelayer PLOVER and converted train ferries. In 1940 she laid mines around the Orkneys and in the St. George's Channel, but was herself mined off Liverpool on 16 January 1941. In July 1941 she took mines to Russia. In 1942, when this picture was taken, she reinforced the East Coast barrier and later took urgently needed depth charges to Gibraltar. In April 1943 she intercepted the German blockade runner IRENE, homeward bound from Japan, which scuttled herself. The next year she was converted to a landing craft repair ship and took part in the Normandy landings. She was sold in 1947.

AMBUSCADE

The AMBUSCADE was a special build by Yarrow, being launched in January 1926. She was readily recognised by her long forecastle even though by the time this photograph was taken (in 1943) she had been modified to meet the needs of the war, with her mainmast reduced and radar fitted above her bridge. Of greatest interest is the squid mortar fitted in place of A gun. She had been employed on the trials of various anti-submarine weapons in 1942-43. The squid mortar proved very successful, the weapon later coming into service with the Castle Class corvettes and Loch Class frigates. In May 1945 the AMBUSCADE was allocated for target trials and was later broken up at Troon in 1947.

ANSON

The battleship ANSON was completed in June 1945 by Swan Hunter and immediately employed covering convoys to Russia, and in strikes against enemy shiping off the Norwegian Coast. After two years of this arduous duty she sailed for the Mediterranean to work up for service in the Far East. She was part of the force that relieved Hong Kong in August 1945, and later was the guardship at Tokyo. She returned to the UK, via Australia, and served in the Training Squadron for three years before being laid up in the Gareloch. She arrived at Faslane in December 1957 for breaking up. Of interest in this photograph are her secondary armament directors, which were of a more modern type than those of her sisters.

H.M.S. ANSON
1945

ARIADNE

The fast minelayer ARIADNE was launched at Stephen's yard in February 1943 and is photographed just after completion in September of that year. She was a repeat of the successful Latona Class, but mounted two twin 4 inch guns instead of three twin 4.7 inch. She could carry 160 mines and her engines (driving two shafts) gave her a top speed of 40 knots. She served in the Mediterranean and then went to the Far East via Panama and Australia. She returned via Pearl Habour and Panama early in 1945, and rejoined the Home Fleet to help escort Crown Prince Olaf of Norway to Oslo in May 1945. She returned to the Far East, via Suez, in July 1945. When she returned to the UK she was placed in reserve until she was broken up in February 1965.

ARTIFEX

The ARTIFEX had been the liner AURANIA, until converted and taken into use as an armed merchant cruiser. She was torpedoed in November 1941 and later that month was taken in hand by Devonport Dockyard for conversion to a heavy repair ship. Her name was changed on 12 November 1942. She commissioned on 5 April 1944 and sailed for the East Indies, and was at Hong Kong by December 1945. She is photographed in her repair ship guise, with light anti-aircraft guns and cranes forward and aft. She returned to the UK to become a harbour training ship for artificer apprentices attached to HMS CALEDONIA at Rosyth, until she was sold in December 1960.

AVENGER

The AVENGER was an auxiliary aircraft carrier, built by the Sun Shipbuilding Company as the RIO HUDSON and launched in November 1940. She commissioned on 2 March 1943 and six months later was part of the substantial escort given to convoy PQ18 to Russia after the heavy losses sustained by the previous convoy, PQ17. Her aircraft sank U589 during this duty, and were invaluable in combating enemy aircraft. She was diesel engined, but as the engines of these early aircraft carrier conversions proved unreliable, later escort carriers were built with geared turbines. She had only a half deck hangar under the after end of the flight deck, but carried 15 aircraft. She was sunk by U155 on 15 November 1942 West of Gibraltar. The previous AVENGER, an armed merchant cruiser, was sunk by the previous U155 also West of Gibraltar - in June 1917.

BARFLEUR

The Battle Class destroyer BARFLEUR was the leader of her class, and was completed by Swan Hunter in September 1944. This early completion allowed her to serve in the Pacific during the war, the only Battle so to do. She was present at the Japanese surrender ceremony in Tokyo Bay in September 1945. She is photographed on 21 January 1945, in her home fleet colours just prior to sailing for the Far East. Serving with the British Pacific Fleet she wore the pennant number D61. This class re-introduced twin gun mountings for destroyers and despite her size (2,325 tons) BARFLEUR achieved 31.65 knots on trials. The single 4 inch gun abaft her funnel was for starshell work, and was later replaced by two single 40 mm guns for anti-aircraft work. She finally paid off in 1958 and was broken up in September 1966.

BARITONE

The boom defence vessel BARITONE was launched in March 1945 by Philip of Dartmouth. Of 730 tons and with a specially rounded stern for working her kedge anchor and cable, she was capable of a 70 ton lift on her forward horns. She is photographed fitted with 3 inch gun aft, with (unusually) no smoke visible from her funnel, as the class were coal burners! She was sold to Pounds at Portsmouth in May 1958.

BELFAST

The cruiser BELFAST was originally designed to carry quadruple 6 inch gun mountings, but ballistic problems led to her carrying the triple 6 inch turrets on a long hull. Being beamier than the Southampton Class, she could carry extra deck and side armour. Commissioned in August 1939, she was nearly sunk by a magnetic mine in the Firth of Forth three months later. She is photographed just after the completion of repairs - which took until October 1942. She was fitted with radar and still carried all six twin 4 inch AA guns. In December 1943 she was part of the force that sank the German battlecruiser SCHARNHORST off North Cape. After service as the flagship of Force E at Normandy, she served in the Far East both during the war and for several commissions afterwards. She was modernised in 1956-59 and was towed to London in October 1971, where she became a permanent museum ship.

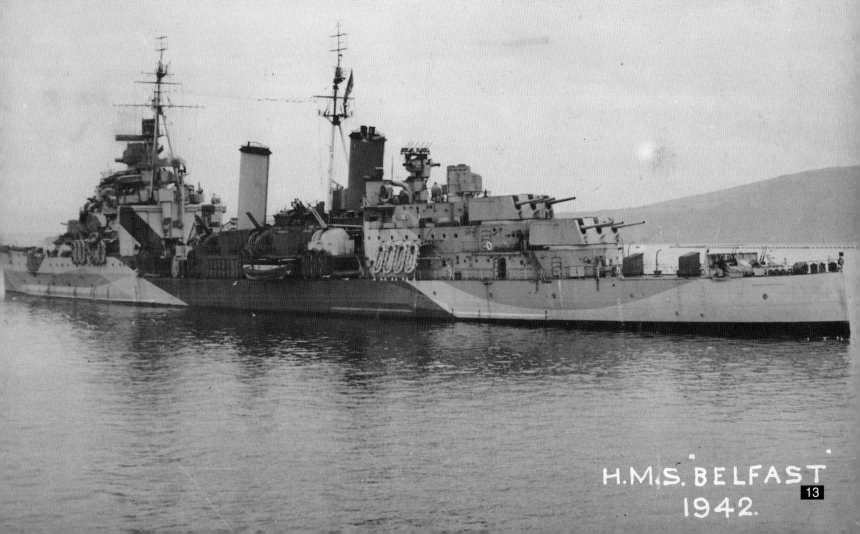

H.M.S. BELFAST
1942.

13

H.M.T. "BERN."
OCT. 2-1942.

BERN

The Isles class trawler BERN was built by Cook, Welton and Gemmel and launched in October 1942. She carried a 12 pounder gun forward and had 20 mm guns aft and by the bridge. She was also armed with depth charges. She operated from Milford Haven until 1944 and with the Eastern Task Force at Normandy and then served in the Channel. In June 1945 she was converted to a wreck dispersal vessel at Aberdeen and in 1956 was converted again for tank cleaning duties. She was sold in July 1958 being broken up at Sittingbourne.

BERRY HEAD

The BERRY HEAD was an escort maintenance ship being launched at Vancouver in October 1944. She was accepted in June 1945 and is photographed a month later. She was sent to Hong Kong, via Australia, arriving in October 1945. In February 1946, she left Hong Kong, via Suez, for the UK, before being placed in reserve at Sheerness in April 1946. She remained there until 1952, when she moved to Devonport, still in reserve, for a few years prior to being modernised with lattice masts and modern AA guns. She replaced TRIUMPH in the Far East in 1969, and in 1970 returned to the UK where she became an accommodation ship at Devonport until 1988. She was then de-equipped prior to her sale in March 1990.

BERWICK

The BERWICK was of the KENT group of County Class cruisers, being completed by Fairfield in February 1928. By 1942, when this photograph was taken, her aircraft had been removed and she was fitted with radar and tripod masts, whilst still retaining her four twin 8 inch turrets and distinctive high sided appearance. In November 1940 she had escorted the raid on Taranto, and later that month was damaged by Italian cruisers during the action off Cape Spartivento. On Christmas Day 1940, she was in action with the German cruiser ADMIRAL HIPPER whilst defending a convoy NW of the Azores and was again hit by 8 inch shellfire. Repairs took until June 1941. She then joined the Home Fleet escorting Russian convoys. On 30 May 1945, she led a force to Trondheim to take over and transfer surrendered U-boats. After the war she was laid up and eventually sold in June 1948.

H.M.S. "BERWICK"
1942.

BIRMINGHAM

Built at Devonport Dockyard and completed in November 1937 the BIRMINGHAM was a Southampton Class cruiser armed with twelve 6 inch guns. She was the only one of the class built without a knuckle in her bow (as an experiment to improve seakeeping qualities.) She was on the China Station until early 1940, when she joined the Home Fleet. She later returned to the Eastern Fleet, being detached to escort convoys to Malta. She was refitted, and in November 1943, two months after this photograph was taken, she was torpedoed by U407 in the Mediterranean whilst returning to the Eastern Fleet. She was hit abreast B turret and lost 70 men. Repairs took until 1945. She later took part in the Korean War and served on the Home and Mediterranean Stations prior to her sale in June 1970.

BRITOMART

The BRITOMART was built at Devonport Dockyard, being completed in August 1939. She was a Halcyon Class minesweeper of 875 tons, originally fitted with two single 4 inch guns. She served in Arctic waters, being one of the escorts that stood by convoy PQ17 when the destroyer escort was withdrawn. Later she returned to home waters and is photographed here at Plymouth in 1944. On 27 August of that year she, with five sister vessels, was operating off the French coast when she was attacked by RAF Typhoon aircraft. BRITOMART was sunk and her Commanding Officer and 21 others lost. (The HUSSAR was also badly hit and had to be sunk, whilst the SALAMANDER had her stern blown off and the JASON damaged.)

H.M.S. BRITOMART.
1944.

BYMS 46

One hundred and fifty of these vessels were built under the lease-lend agreement with the USA during the war. They were all wooden construction vessels of 292-335 tons and their two (diesel driven) propellers could give them 14 knots. They were armed with a 3 inch gun and could operate Oropesa wire and influence sweeps. BYMS 46 was built by Gibbs Jackson of Florida and completed in February 1943. She served in West African waters and later in the Channel and at Ostend. She finally docked and refitted at Ghent, where she paid off on 16 May 1945, for transfer to the Royal Netherlands Navy as the WESTERSCHELDE. She was deleted in 1958.

CAESAR

The leader of the Ca Class of destroyers, CAESAR was originally to have been named RANGER. She was completed by John Brown in October 1944 and is photographed three months later entering Devonport. She served with the Home Fleet and then transferred to the Far East. She was fitted with a single heavy director on the bridge and had four single 4.5 inch guns. Later C Class groups had the bigger Mk 6 director and, after the war, CAESAR and her sisters were refitted to match. In 1957-60 she was again refitted with a newer (Mk 6M) director and enclosed bridge. She was broken up where she was built, on the Clyde, arriving there in January 1967.

H.M.S. "CAESAR" 1945

CARLISLE

The CARLISLE was in the last group of the C Class of cruisers, being built by Fairfield and completed in November 1918, with five 6 inch guns. In 1939 she was modernised to become an AA cruiser, with four twin 4 inch guns, a pom pom in B position and other smaller weapons. Such ships were in great demand and she served off Norway in 1940, bearing the brunt of the bombing at Molde and Aandalsnes, and then transferred to the Mediterranean. She was at the evacuation of Greece and Crete, her Captain being killed during the latter operation. At one point she was running on only one shaft, as she could not be released for repairs. She escorted convoys to Malta and was at the Second Battle of Sirte. She was refitted at Devonport from July 1942-March 1943. In October 1943 she was hit off Leros with the loss of 20 lives. She had to be towed to Alexandria and was then used as a base ship. She was broken up in 1949.

H.M.S. CARLISLE

CENTURION

The battleship CENTURION was launched at Devonport Dockyard in November 1911. After service in the First World War (which included being at Jutland) she took part in operations in the Black Sea prior to being converted to a target ship. In 1941 she was again converted, this time to a dummy of the battleship ANSON, in which guise she is photographed off Plymouth. She then sailed for Alexandria via the Cape. During heavy weather in the Indian Ocean she lost her A turret, and it is reported that one lookout in the convoy was amazed when he had to report a 14 inch gun floating past his ship. She was fitted with AA guns to escort a convoy to Malta, during which she was hit by bombs. Because of the damage sustained and her general condition she became an AA battery at Suez. In 1944 she returned to Devonport to be fitted out as a blockship and was sunk as part of the harbour at Omaha Beach off Normandy on 9 June 1944.

CLEVELAND

The CLEVELAND was completed at Yarrow in September 1940. She was in the first group of the Hunt Class escort destroyers, carrying two twin 4 inch guns with a pom pom in X position. She was also fitted with an extra 2 pounder right forward in the bows for use against enemy E-boats. These vessels were to have had three twin 4 inch mountings, but this was found to make them top heavy. Although of only 907 tons, these ships were designed for 30 knots, and were employed alongside larger fleet destroyers. She was one of the covering force for the St. Nazaire raid in March 1942. She was at the Salerno and South of France landings, later being part of the force re-occupying the Aegean Islands and Greek mainland. She was wrecked on her way to the breaker's yard in June 1957, her hull being blown up on Rhossili Sands in December 1959.

DACRES

Built in Boston USA the DACRES was commissioned in August 1943. She was one of the 'short' Captain Class destroyer escorts built for the Royal Navy, having a two shaft diesel electric propulsion giving her 20 knots. It had been planned to double the horse power of this class, but instead it was decided to halve the engines in each vessel and build more hulls. DACRES was fitted as a small headquarters ship for combined operations, with her after 3 inch and twin 40 mm guns removed and a mast fitted for extra communications equipment. She was used in this role in the Normandy Landings in Area Sword until 1 October 1944 and was later at Rouen. She was returned to the US Navy at Boston on 28 January 1946.

DELHI

Built by Armstrong Walker, being completed in June 1919, the DELHI was a D Class cruiser fitted with six 6 inch guns and twelve torpedo tubes. At the outbreak of war she served in the Home and then Mediterranean Fleets prior to being refitted at New York Navy Yard and Devonport Dockyard with American 5 inch guns and directors. Her new armament and tripod masts are shown clearly in this photograph, taken in 1942, just after her refit. She went on to serve in Home and Mediterranean waters again until she was badly damaged at Split on 12 February 1945. She was towed back to Britain but repairs were never completed. She arrived at Newport in March 1948 to be broken up.

H.M.S. DELHI
1942

DIDO

The DIDO was nameship of her class of light cruisers built with 5.25 inch guns to avoid the mix of 6 inch and 4 inch guns fitted in previous cruiser classes. She is photographed here in the Firth of Forth shortly after completion in September 1940, with only four of her five twin turrets. She had a single 4 inch in Q position for starshell work, the fifth turret being fitted later in the war. She was bombed off Crete during the evacuation, 103 of the 240 Black Watch soldiers onboard being killed, together with 46 of her crew. After repairs at Brooklyn she returned to the Mediterranean and took part in the Second Battle of Sirte and later operated from North African ports. She returned to Home waters in 1944, escorting Russian convoys and taking part in operations off the Norwegian Coast. She took the surrender of Copenhagen on 9 May 1945. After the war she was placed in reserve and was broken up at Barrow in July 1958.

DUKE OF YORK

The King George V Class battleship DUKE OF YORK was built on the Clyde by John Brown and completed in November 1941. The next month she took Winston Churchill to America, and was then employed guarding Russian convoys, and in strikes against Norwegian coastal shipping. On 26 December 1943 she was flagship of the force that sank the battlecruiser SCHARNHORST off North Cape. The DUKE OF YORK's gunfire slowed the German ship and allowed cruisers and destroyers to close and launch their torpedoes. After a refit at Liverpool in late 1944, she transferred to the British Pacific Fleet and was at Tokyo Bay for the Japanese surrender ceremony in 1945. After the war she served with the Home Fleet and was placed in reserve in 1949, being broken up at Faslane in February 1958.

EREBUS

The monitor EREBUS is photographed here steaming at what appears to be her top speed of 14 knots on her way back to the UK to refit after Operation Husky. She had been built at Govan, (completed in September 1916) and was then employed in the Channel where she was damaged by a German motor boat off Ostend. Between the wars she was a gunnery training ship, but in 1940 was using her twin 15 inch guns to bombard German positions in France and Belgium. She then went to the Indian Ocean, where she was damaged by Japanese aircraft in April 1942. She entered the Mediterranean in June 1943 and took part in the Sicilian landings. Afterwards she was at the Normandy landings, where she was damaged by a miss-fire, and later by shellfire from ashore. After assisting at Walcheren, she became a turret drill ship before being broken up in January 1947.

FISHGUARD

The FISHGUARD was one of ten US Coast Guard cutters transferred to the Royal Navy. She had been called the TAHOE and was launched at Bethlehem in 1927. These ships had two shaft turbo electric propulsion giving them 16 knots, and they were armed with a single 5 inch, two 3 inch and several smaller guns. They were not built as warships and lacked watertight subdivision. One vessel was torpedoed and sank in two minutes. FISHGUARD served on North and South Atlantic convoy duty and also in the Mediterranean for the Sicilian landings. Later she was in the Indian Ocean and helped salvage equipment from U852 which had been forced to scuttle herself off the Somali Coast. She returned to Portsmouth in December 1945 and was returned to the USA in February 1946.

FLAMBOROUGH HEAD

The FLAMBOROUGH HEAD was an escort maintenance vessel launched at Vancouver in October 1944. Her standard Empire ship lines can be seen in this photograph, (taken in May 1945) and her covered oerlikon gun barrels look odd in their vertical stowage. She was commissioned in May 1945 but paid off a year later. In 1948-49 she was used as an accommodation ship for target trials and was transferred to the Royal Canadian Navy on 2 May 1951, being renamed CAPE BRETON. She served at Halifax and at Esquimalt.

FOXTROT

The trawlers used by the Navy were very versatile and FOXTROT of the Dance Class was photographed in January 1943 in her anti-submarine role. She was launched by Cochrane in April 1940 and carried a 4 inch gun forward in addition to three 20 mm guns. She was damaged when rammed by a merchant ship in February 1941. In April 1943 she entered the Mediterranean and remained there until transferred to the RASC on 23 May 1945. In her latter days she was used on wreck dispersal duties before being broken up in September 1951.

FROBISHER

The FROBISHER was built as a trade protection cruiser, being launched at Devonport Dockyard in March 1920. She was armed with seven single 7.5 inch guns, some of which were landed when she became a training ship between the wars. She was rearmed during a refit at Devonport which lasted until February 1942, when this picture was taken, and she was then employed on the trade routes with the Eastern Fleet. She returned to the UK to act as a bombarding ship at Normandy, where she was also used as a depot ship for small craft. On 8 August 1944 she was damaged by a torpedo off the French coast. She was repaired and reverted to being a training ship for officer cadets, before paying off in March 1947 and being broken up at Newport in May 1949.

GARDENIA

The GARDENIA was one of the first Flower Class corvettes, being completed in April 1940, two weeks after the first of the class. She is photographed still wearing the original M pennant number, later changed to K. She was one of the original design with a short forecastle and with the foremast stepped forward of the bridge. 280 of this class were ordered. She was used on convoy protection duty, and was one of the escorts of convoy HG76 (from Gibraltar in December 1941) when the carrier AUDACITY was lost but four U-boats sunk. She was lost in a collision with the trawler FLUELLEN off Oran on 9 November 1942.

M99

GARLAND

The destroyer GARLAND was built by Fairfield, being completed in March 1936. She was originally fitted with four 4.7 inch guns, and two sets of quadruple torpedo tubes. By 1942 when this photograph was taken, she had been modified for escort duty. She was transferred to the Polish Navy in 1939. In September 1939 she was damaged in a depth charge explosion whilst on convoy duty in the Mediterranean. Repairs took until April 1940. She joined Western Approaches Command in September 1940, escorting Atlantic and Russian convoys. Whilst escorting PQ16 on 23 May 1942 she was bombed and splinters swept her decks killing 8 and wounding 40. Repairs took four months. She later returned to the Mediterranean and helped to sink U407 North of Crete in September 1944. She remained Polish until 1947. She then became the Dutch MARNIX until April 1964, when she was broken up at Antwerp.

GREY RANGER

The GREY RANGER presented an odd appearance carrying a dummy funnel forward and with canvas rigged to make her look more like a freighter than an oiler. Tanker tonnage was very scarce during the war, and every effort was made to hide these vessels in convoy. GREY RANGER was built by Caledon in 1941 and was fitted with the first successful self tensioning winch for use in replenishment at sea. In December 1941 she supported the raid on the Lofotens. Whilst with Russian convoy QP14 on 22 September 1942, she was torpedoed and her engines damaged, and had to be sunk by friendly forces.

GREY SHARK

GREY SHARK was a steam gun boat of 165 tons, originally listed as SGB 6. She is photographed with a reduced gunnery armament to allow her to carry torpedo tubes. These craft were named in 1943 when it was realised that they were just long enough, at 145, feet to qualify for names. Their steam machinery proved vulnerable to gunfire, and armour plate had to be added, reducing their speed from 35 to 27 knots. GREY SHARK was launched by Hawthorn Leslie in November 1941 and served in the Channel, including the Normandy Landings. She was sold in October 1947.

HART

The HART was a modified Black Swan Class sloop completed by
Stephen in December 1943. This class carried three twin 4 inch
gun mountings, but unlike earlier sloops, carried only light guns on
their quarterdecks to make room for more depth charge throwers
and racks. They were slightly beamier too, had an extra half knot in
speed, and were fitted with Denny Brown "roll reducers". HART
helped sink U482 in the North Channel on 16 January 1945. In
September 1945 she was part of the force that took the Japanese
surrender in the Bismarck Islands and New Guinea. She remained
in the Far East until 1952, taking part in the Korean War. In May
1959 she was transferred to the German Navy and was renamed
SCHEER, before being broken up in 1969.

HECLA

The HECLA was a destroyer depot ship and sister to the TYNE. Completed by Clydebank in December 1940, her early career included supplying bread to Greenock for four days when that town was badly damaged by air raids. Apart from being able to supply 6,000 pounds of bread a day, she had 20,000 sq. ft. of workshops and a large capacity to produce elecricity and water. She is photographed at Iceland supporting escorts - the destroyer ORIBI and the Canadian corvettes ARROWHEAD and BADDECK are amongst those alongside. She sailed for the Eastern Fleet in May 1942, but was mined off Cape Agulhas with the loss of 24 men with many injured. After repairs she sailed again, but was torpedoed, by U515, off Cape St Vincent on 12 November 1942 and was lost.

HOWE

The King George V Class battleship HOWE is seen here in the Firth of Forth just after her completion, by Fairfield, in August 1942. She was on her way to Scapa Flow for trials and working up. Her ten 14 inch guns can be seen here, the quadruple turrets weighed 1,500 tons, and the twin in B position 900 tons. Her broadside weighed 1,590 pounds. She provided protection to Russian convoys, and in 1943 supported the invasions of Sicily and Italy. After a refit at Devonport in 1944, she became the Flagship of the British Pacific Fleet, bombarding Sumatra and later Miyako. After the war she served in the Training Squadron and was then laid up at Devonport until being broken up at Inverkeithing in May 1958.

ICARUS

The destroyer ICARUS was launched at Clydebank in November 1936. She was of the I Class which introduced a new destroyer bridge and quintuple torpedo tubes. On 14 October 1939 she helped sink U45, and on 29th of the next month, helped sink U35. In the spring of 1940 she laid mines off Norway, and then took part in the Second Battle of Narvik. She was damaged by bombing whilst assisting in the evacuation of Dunkirk, where she rescued over 4,700 troops. The next year she was part of the HOOD's escort when the BISMARCK broke out into the Atlantic. In 1941-45 she escorted convoys to Russia and Malta as well as being in North Atlantic Support Groups. On 6 March 1944 she helped sink U744 (after a 30 hour hunt) and on 21 January 1945 helped sink U1199 off Land's End. She was broken up at Troon in October 1946, ten years after her launch.

INDEFATIGABLE

The INDEFATIGABLE was completed on Clydebank in May 1944. She was in the third group of the Illustrious Class of Fleet aircraft carriers which had a fourth propellor shaft and an extra hangar. Her aircraft carried out strikes against the TIRPITZ and shipping off the Norwegian Coast. In November 1944 she joined the British Pacific Fleet. She was hit by a Kamikaze on 1 April 1945, but was able to continue operating. Her aircraft struck at Pelambang, Sakishima, Okinawa and the Japanese homelands. She was present in Tokyo Bay for the surrender ceremony on 2 September 1945. She later undertook repatriation dutes and joined the Training Squadron and the 1953 Coronation Review at Spithead. She was broken up at Dalmuir and Troon in 1956/7.

INDOMITABLE

The INDOMITABLE was completed by Vickers Armstrong in October 1941 and differed from earlier half sisters in the Illustrious Class in having an extra half hangar. She ran aground in the West Indies which delayed her work up, but arrived in the Indian Ocean in January 1942, just after the Japanese had started their major advance. She took part in the Madagascar Operation in May 1942, and entered the Mediterranean for the Pedestal convoy in August that year, when she was badly damaged. Whilst supporting the Sicilian landings in July 1943, she was hit by an aerial torpedo and again suffered severe damage. Later she served in the Eastern and British Pacific Fleets, taking part in operations against Pelambang and Okinawa. She was hit by a Kamikaze on 4 May 1945, but continued to operate aircraft. She was modernised after the war and was Home Fleet Flagship in 1951-52. She arrived at Faslane for breaking up in September 1955.

JAVELIN

The JAVELIN had been laid down by John Brown as the KASHMIR, but her name was changed before her launch on 21 December 1938. The J Class destroyers were fine looking vessels with a powerful gun armament of three twin 4.7 inch guns - and ten torpedo tubes. Their weakness lay in their AA capability. JAVELIN lost two men in a collision with a merchant ship in October 1939, and 43 killed when her bow and stern were blown off during an action with German destroyers in the Channel in November 1940. She later served in the Indian Ocean, the Mediterranean and took part in Channel operations during the Normandy Landings. She was one of the two of her class to survive the war later to be broken up (at Troon) in November 1949.

K235

K235

JED

This photograph of the River Class frigate JED was taken just after she had been completed, at Bristol, in November 1942. With two propellor shafts and with a sea speed of 18 knots, these vessels were better equipped for North Atlantic escort duty than the earlier corvettes. They were armed with two single 4 inch guns, a hedge-hog anti-submarine mortar and a heavy depth charge armament. The first 24 of this class were fitted for minesweeping. JED was employed in the North Atlantic support groups and assisted the PELICAN in the sinking of U438 on 6 May 1943. She also helped sink U954 on 19 May 1943 and U334 on 14 June that year. In 1945 she served in the Indian Ocean, but on return to the UK in December 1945 was placed in reserve. She was broken up at Milford Haven in July 1957.

JERVIS

The JERVIS is photographed here in June 1945, showing remarkably few alterations to her original appearance. She had a lattice foremast instead of a tripod, and had been fitted with radar, but her main armament remained unchanged. She was leader of the J Class, launched by Hawthorn Leslie on 9 September 1938. She took part in the Battle of Matapan in March 1941, sinking the Italian cruiser POLA. She was part of the force that prevented the German seaborne landings on Crete in May 1941. Six months later she was damaged at Alexandria when the oiler she was alongside was mined. Her bow was damaged when she was hit by a glider bomb off Anzio but later took part in the Normandy Landings in June 1944. She was used for explosive trials in 1945 before being broken up at Troon in January 1949.

JUNON

The JUNON was a French Diane Class coastal submarine launched by Normand on 15 September 1935 and completed the following year. She displaced 579 tons and carried a 3 inch gun, seven 21.7 inch and two 15.7 inch torpedo tubes. When France fell to Germany, she was taken under Royal Naval operational control. She helped patrol off Brest in March 1941, when the German heavy units were there, and the next year carried out patrols off Norway. She broke down at sea in March 1942 and repairs took five months due to the difficulty in obtaining spares. She continued to operate from Dundee until 1944. In May 1944 she called at Gibraltar and Algiers, and was placed in special reserve at Oran in August 1944, where it was found repairs would take several months. There were 22 in her class, four of which became war losses, and one was wrecked. By 1952 JUNON was the sole survivor - as a training ship.

H.M.S. JUNON
1941.

KENT

The KENT was the nameship of the first group of the County Class of cruisers, with eight 8 inch guns. She was built by Chatham Dockyard, being completed in June 1928. Before the war she served on the China Station, although she returned for a refit in 1937-38. She was on the East Indies Station in 1939-40, but had joined the Mediterranean Fleet by June 1940. She was damaged by an aerial torpedo off Bardia in September 1940 and steamed to Devonport for repairs. Whilst there she was damaged by a bomb. This photograph was taken in 1941, just after her repairs and before she headed North to cover Russian convoys and strikes against shipping off the Norwegian coast. She had radar fitted and extra anti-aircraft guns, but still carried her aircraft. She was placed in reserve in 1945 and was broken up at Troon in 1948.

H.M.S. KENT.
1941

KINTERBURY

The naval armament carrier KINTER-BURY was photographed just after completion by Philip of Dartmouth in 1943. She had a deadweight capacity of 600 tons. She displaced 1,488 tons, and was coal fired. During the war she was defensively armed as can be seen in this photograph. She served for a long period, moving armaments between naval ports, before being sold in August 1978, for breaking up.

H.M.S. KINTERBURY

KUJAWIAK

The Polish KUJAWIAK was a Hunt Class escort destroyer built by Vickers Armstrong as the OAKLEY. She was launched in October 1940 and handed over to the Poles before completion. Of the second group of the Hunt Class, she carried three twin 4 inch guns, being 2.5 feet beamier and more stable than the first group. She mounted a quadruple 2 pounder abaft her funnel. In June 1941 she was damaged by an aircraft which attacked her with machine guns. In December 1941 she was in a force that raided the Lofotens. In March 1942 she suffered casualties when attacked by several aircraft. In June 1942 she escorted a convoy to Malta (Operation Harpoon) which was heavily attacked by aircraft, submarines and surface vessels. She was mined off Malta on 15th on the last leg of this operation, and sank under tow the next day.

H.M.S. "KRUJAWIAK"
1941

LEANDER

The LEANDER was the nameship of a class of light cruisers with a distinctive single funnel profile. She was launched at Devonport Dockyard on 24 September 1931 and became part of the New Zealand Division in April 1937. She served in the Indian Ocean and Red Sea during the early years of the war. At the time this photograph was taken (October 1942) she retained her original pole masts, four twin 6 inch turrets and aircraft, but her single 4 inch AA guns had been replaced by twin mountings. On 13 July 1943 she was torpedoed at the Battle of Kolombangara, losing 3 killed and 24 missing, and having a hole 9 by 6 metres in her forward boiler room. Temporary repairs were carried out at Auckland, she then sailed for Boston and the UK for more permanent work. She was returned to the Royal Navy in 1943. In 1946 she served in the Mediterranean prior to being used on trials. She was broken up at Blyth in January 1950.

LEWES

The LEWES was one of the fifty US destroyers transferred to the Royal Navy in 1940. She had already been deleted from the US Navy lists prior to transfer, and was given a temporary name (CONWAY) in place of her original name (CRAVEN) which had already been re-allocated. She commissioned at Halifax in October 1940 and arrived at Devonport for refit in November. She was bombed whilst refitting and did not enter service until February 1942 - the last of the 50 to become fully oprational. Ten months later she was refitted as an air target ship and served in the East Indies and off New South Wales. Her forward 3 inch gun was replaced by two single 2 pounders on the forecastle and she had a distinctively shaped bridge. She paid off at Sydney in November 1945, the last "four stacker" so to do, her hull was stripped and she was scuttled off Sydney on 25 May 1946.

H.M.S. LEWES.

LIFELINE

The LIFELINE was a coastal salvage vessel of 950 tons, launched by Smith's Dock in August 1943. These vessels were used to keep the esturial waters clear of the many wrecks that impeded navigation, an essential and dangerous task in wartime. She carried a single oerlikon on each bridge wing, and her quick release life-saving floats are conspicuous in the photograph, as are her kedge anchors. She was chartered to a private firm from 1947-60 and was sold in 1960, eventually being broken up in April 1981.

LIMBOURNE

The LIMBOURNE was completed by Alex Stephen in October 1942 and was in the third group of Hunt Class escort destroyers, having two twin 4 inch guns and a quadruple 2 pounder abaft the funnel. She also had two 21 inch torpedo tubes, reflecting the amount of work these small vessels were expected to do with the larger fleet destroyers. In December 1942 she joined the 15th Destroyer Flotilla based at Devonport. This photograph was taken a month later in Plymouth Sound. In October 1943 she took part in a sweep of the North Coast of Brittany with the cruiser CHARYBDIS and several other destroyers. The force was attacked by German destroyers, the CHARYBDIS was sunk and the LIMBOURNE's bow blown off. She later had to be sunk by the destroyer ROCKET - on the eve of the anniversary of her coming into service.

LOCH GORM

The LOCH GORM was launched by Harland and Wolff in June 1944 and completed on the Clyde. The Loch Class frigates were based on the River Class design, but with hull sections that could be assembled in yards used for mercantile building as, by 1943, much mercantile construction was being undertaken abroad. This class was fitted with a double squid anti-submarine mortar in B position, and hence the relatively clear quarterdeck without the clutter of depth charge throwers and rails. She served in the East Indies in 1945, arriving at Trincomalee on 22 August. On return to Devonport in September 1946 she was placed in reserve. Sold in 1961 she became a Greek passenger ferry (named ORION) being broken up in Yugoslavia five years later.

LORD INCHCAPE

The LORD INCHCAPE was one of many trawlers requisitioned (for minesweeping duties) just before the outbreak of war. She had been launched in 1924 and was of 338 tons. She took part in the Dunkirk evacuation but was damaged by a mine on 25 October 1940, sinking in 24 feet of water in Jennycliff Bay (Plymouth) after a tow. She lost one seaman. She was raised on 27 January 1942 and repaired over two months. She then served in the Channel until being laid up in the Humber in May 1945. This photograph was taken in 1943 after she had returned to service and shows her light defensive armament, low freeboard, and classic tall bridge structure. An accoustic sweep can be seen on her forecastle. She was sold in October, 1948.

H.M.T. LORD INCHCAPE

LOYAL

The LOYAL was completed by Scotts in December 1942. The L Class destroyers were the first fitted with three power operated turrets, each of twin 4.7 inch guns. Immediately after work up she and her sister ship, LIGHTNING, were in action sinking two Italian ships in the Gulf of Gabes. Two months later she had to rescue 181 survivors from the LIGHTNING when an E boat sank her. She took part in the Salerno landings, firing 1714 rounds of 4.7 inch despite being hit in the boiler room. She remained in action for a further three weeks after the damage. At the Anzio landings she was again hit and her engines disabled. Later she was straddled by bombs and had to be refitted at Taranto. On 12 October 1944 she set off a mine which displaced her starboard engine and blew in 160 feet of her side. She was used as a base ship at Malta until 1948, when she was towed to Milford Haven to be broken up.

LST(3) 3036

Launched in November 1944, by Ailsa shipbuilding, LST 3036 was of 2,256 tons and steam driven, as no suitable diesel engines were available for these landing ships. The stern fitting and machinery for her kedge anchor can be seen in this photograph taken in May 1945. She could carry fifteen 40 ton tanks, or twenty seven 25 ton tanks. She was named PUNCHER in 1947 and, after a long period in reserve, was sold for breaking up, arriving in Ghent in June 1961.

LYDD

The LYDD, ex LYDNEY, was a Later Hunt Class minesweeper, launched by Fairfield in December 1918. These ships were armed with one 4 inch and one 3 inch gun, had coal burning boilers, which earned them the nickname "Smokey Joes". They could make 16 knots. LYDD took part in the Dunkirk evacuation and also the Normandy Landings. At the end of the war she was in the Fourth Minesweeping Flotilla at Plymouth, before being placed in reserve. She was sold in March 1947 to a Belgian company for mercantile use.

MAHRATTA

The M Class destroyer MAHRATTA was launched on 28 July 1942 -
later than scheduled as she had been blown off the stocks during an
air raid whilst building at Scotts. She was originally to have been
called MARKSMAN. Completed in March 1943, when this photograph was taken, showing her graceful lines, power operated turrets
and single director, she served in northern waters. She was torpedoed
by U990 in the Barents Sea on 25 February 1944 whilst escorting convoy JW57. She was first hit at 2100 and brought to a standstill. A second torpedo hit five minutes later and flooded her after engine room,
possibly blowing off her stern. The destroyer IMPULSIVE tried to go
alongside her in a snowstorm, but at 2232 the MAHRATTA rolled over
and sank. Only 17 of her crew were rescued from the icy waters.

MALAYA

The battleship MALAYA was launched in 1915 at Elswick, and lost 63 men killed at the Battle of Jutland. Between the wars she was modernised and given an improved AA armament, but did not receive the radical updating that some of her sisters were given. She carried out bombardments in the Mediterranean and also escorted convoys. In March 1941 she sighted the SCHARNHORST and GNEISENAU whilst on the latter duty. Later that month she was torpedoed off Cape Verde. She was repaired in the USA, the first ship to be refitted under the Lease Lend agreement. After refit she continued on convoy escort work until paying off in December 1943. She was recommissioned for bombarding duties in June 1944, and then became part of the VERNON training establishment at Portsmouth during 1945-47. She was broken up at Faslane in April 1948.

MALCOLM

The flotilla leader MALCOLM was completed by Cammell Laird in 1919 and was originally armed with five 4.7 inch guns, a single 3 inch gun and two triple 21 inch torpedo tubes. She was of the Campbell Class, designed to lead the V & W Class destroyers. She took part in the Dunkirk evacuation, where she was damaged, and in August 1940, sank two German ships off the Texel. By 1942, when this photograph was taken, her gunnery and torpedo armament had been reduced to allow her to be fitted with a radar on the bridge and enhanced anti-submarine weapons. She was then classified as a short range escort. During convoy duties she helped sink U651 South of Iceland on 29 June 1941. She also escorted the carrier FURIOUS taking aircraft to Malta in August 1942, and during the next month was part of the strong escort given to the Russian convoy PQ18. In November 1942 she was the only ship to survive the unsuccessful attempt to enter Algiers harbour. She was broken up at Barrow in July 1945.

H.M.S. MALCOLM.
1942

61

MAURITIUS

The MAURITIUS was one of the Colony Class cruisers, being launched by Swan Hunter in July 1939. She served in the Atlantic and then East Indies, before joining the 15th Cruiser Squadron in the Mediterranean in 1943. She did not fire a shot in anger until the landings at Sicily. She also supported the landings at Salerno and Anzio before returning to home waters in 1944. She took part in the Normandy Landings and then carried out patrols in the Bay of Biscay, sinking two enemy minesweepers and three trawlers in August 1944. In late 1944 she operated off the Norwegian coast, engaging four enemy destroyers off Bergen on 28 January 1945. damaging one and driving them all back to harbour. She was then refitted, and her X turret removed. This refit did not complete until 1946. She went on to serve in the Mediterranean and East Indies prior to being placed in reserve in 1953. She arrived at Inverkeithing for breaking up in March 1965.

MENELAUS

The MENELAUS was launched as the monitor M31 by Harland and Wolff in June 1915. She was armed with two 6 inch guns from the Queen Elizabeth Class battleships. In 1919 she was converted to a minelayer and renamed MELPOMENE in 1925. She became a tender to the Torpedo School DEFIANCE at Devonport, and was renamed MENELAUS in 1940. This photograph shows her with a single torpedo tube on the forecastle and with mine rails aft for use in her training role. She was sold in 1948. It is hoped (1994) to restore a sister, the M33, (later MINERVA), at Portsmouth.

H.M.S. MENELAUS.
1942

MOTOR FISHING VESSEL

Before the war, motor fishing vessels were used by the Fleet for a variety of tasks, such as landing libertymen or collecting stores. Many of these craft were survivors of the large number of such vessels used in the First World War, but by 1942, more were required, so over a thousand were built. They were of four basic designs, 45 feet, 61.5 feet, 75 feet and 90 feet in length. This photograph shows a 45 feet type, flying the White Ensign and with light guns fore and aft. Many were sold after the war, but some were retained and used until replaced by metal fleet tenders built in the 1960s.

MISTRAL

A French Simoun Class destroyer of 1319 tons, the MISTRAL was launched in June 1925 and carried four single 5.1 inch guns and six 21.7 inch torpedo tubes. During trials she averaged 34 knots - for 12 hours. She served with the French Navy at the Dunkirk evacuation and taken under Royal Naval control on 3 July 1940 at Portsmouth after the fall of France. She was commissioned as a Royal Naval ship in July 1940. She rescued survivors from the Free French torpedo boat BRANLE-BAS that foundered in December 1940, but she was damaged beyond repair by German coastal batteries off France on 10 June 1944. She had been employed as a tender to the gunnery training ship CARDIFF for much fo the war. She was returned to the French Navy in 1946.

MOTOR MINESWEEPER 15

This photograph shows one of the 105 feet type of motor minesweepers, known as "Mickey Mice" - of which 308 were built. They were of wooden construction and could achieve 11 knots. They were adequate for LL sweeping, but not so good with a wire sweep. They had a twin 0.5 inch machine gun mounted on the after end of their superstructure for self defence. Later, they were fitted with acoustic sweeps on the bow, as can be seen in this photograph. Number 15 was completed in March 1941 and is wearing her J pennant number. Later these ships wore their own number on their sides. 1500 was added to their numbers later. She was sold in 1946.

NELSON

The battleship NELSON had been built by Armstrong, completing in June 1927, to a novel design with the aim of containing her nine 16 inch guns in a hull that was within the international treaty limits. Although twelve years old in 1939, and only capable of 23 knots, she played a full part in the war. She was mined in December 1939, as she was entering Loch Ewe, and was hit by a torpedo during a convoy to Malta in Setember 1941. She assisted in the landings at North Africa, Sicily and Salerno, and the Italian armistice was signed onboard her at Malta. She was at the Normandy Landings, where she was again mined. After repairs in the USA she joined the Eastern Fleet and was present at the Japanese surrender at Penang, which was signed onboard, and was later at Singapore. After the war she was used for training, and then as a bombing target before being broken up in 1949.

H.M.S. NEWPC
1941

NEWPORT

The NEWPORT, ex USS SIGOURNAY, was launched in December 1917 and was transferred to the Royal Navy at Halifax in November 1940. The next month she sailed across the Atlantic, was slightly damaged in an air raid at Belfast but broke down on her way to Devonport. On arrival, she was refitted, being lent to the Royal Norwegian Navy in July 1941. She is photographed at that time, with her original bridge and four single 4 inch guns. She served in the 43rd and 7th Escort Groups. In March 1942 she was in collision with the BEVERLEY, and was returned to the Royal Navy before repairs were completed. No longer required as an escort, she became an air target ship in the Western Approaches, paying off in July 1945, and being broken up at Granton in February 1947.

NORLAND

The 393 ton trawler NORLAND was launched in 1916 and was taken as a German prize. She was requisitioned in April 1940, for service as a boom defence vessel and was retained until 1946. She is photographed here in Plymouth Sound, modified to handle the boom wires. She was unarmed.

ZI80

H.M.B.D.V. 'NORDLAND.'
1943

OCEAN

The light fleet carrier OCEAN was of the Colossus Class, being completed by Stephen in June 1945. Completion of this class was delayed by six weeks in order that dining halls could be fitted. The loss of time, and accommodation, was considered well worth the benefits gained. This class had a mercantile hull up to the main deck level with the intention of converting them to commerical use after the war, though all were retained as aircraft carriers. The first jet aircraft deck landings took place onboard her on 4 December 1945 off the Isle of Wight. The subsequent take off was completed using rockets. She later took part in the Korean War and in 1956 embarked troops and equipment for the Suez operation. She was placed in reserve in 1958, and broken up at Faslane in May 1962.

OLNA

The OLNA was built as the Shell tanker HYALINA by Swan Hunter, and completed in 1945. She was immediately taken over by the Admiralty as a fast fleet oiler, being commissioned in the Royal Navy and manned for the British Pacific Fleet. Her turbo electric propulsion could drive her at 17 knots, and her hull was armoured around the fuel tanks. She had a deadweight capacity of 17,500 tons. She was later used for replenishment at sea experiements, and successful ideas were incorporated into the later Tide and O Class oilers. She was broken up in 1966.

"ONSLOW". 10/12/42. 15. KTS.

ONSLOW

The ONSLOW was the leader of the O Class destroyers. Originally armed with four single 4.7 inch guns and eight torpedo tubes, though in this photograph it can be seen that the after tubes and Y gun had been landed, and an extra AA gun fitted in place of the tubes. She was commissioned at Clydebank on 23 September 1941, and served in Arctic waters, helping to sink U88 on 11 September 1942 and U589 three days later. Her most famous action was in December 1942 when she, commanded by Captain Sherbrooke, was one of the destroyers that defended a Russian convoy against the German battleship LUTZOW and heavy cruiser ADMIRAL HIPPER. During the action she was straddled by four shells from the cruiser, both forward guns were put out of action, fires started in the forward superstructure and messdecks, she was holed in the side and splinters swept her bridge. In September 1949 she was transferred to the Royal Pakistan Navy and renamed TIPPU SULTAN.

ORKAN

The ORKAN had been launched by Fairfield in March 1942 as the MYRMIDON, but was completed in December 1942 as the Polish ORKAN. She was of the M Class and is photographed with her after set of quadruple torpedo tubes replaced by an AA gun. She escorted Russian convoys and in July 1943 she brought the body of General Sikorski from Gibraltar (where he had died in an aircraft accident) to Devonport. Later she was employed on escort duty in the North Atlantic and Bay of Biscay. On 7 October 1943, whilst escorting convoy SC143 in the North Atlantic, she attacked U785, which fired a T5 torpedo that exploded in her wake. At 0605 the next day another torpedo, fired by U378, exploded in her wake and, almost immediately afterwards a further torpedo hit her. She sank in three minutes. Forty four survivors were resued by MUSKETEER.

PATHFINDER

The PATHFINDER was launched by Hawthorn Leslie in April 1941. She carried five single 4 inch guns, the supply of 4.7 inch – guns being insufficient for the number of destroyers being built at that time. On 12 August 1942, she helped sink the Italian submarine COBALTO, and a month later helped sink U162 off the Antilles. On 23 April 1943, she again helped to sink U203. Later she was sent to the Eastern Fleet and took part in operations off Burma. In February 1945 she was attacked by Japanese aircraft off Ramree Island and badly damaged. She was towed to the UK and used as an air target. She was broken up at Milford Haven in 1948, her engines being taken to the Royal Naval Engineering College for instructional purposes.

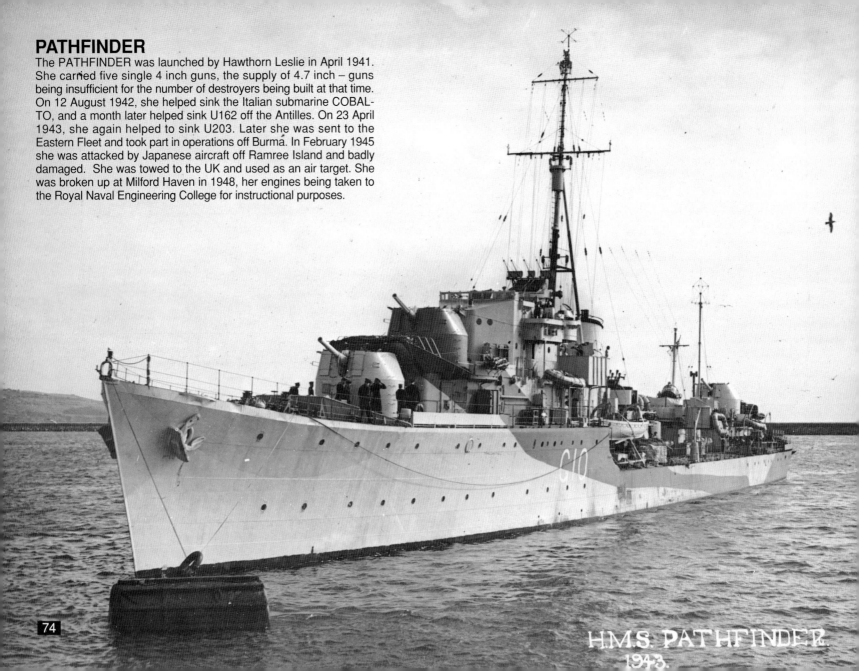

H.M.S. PATHFINDER.
1943.

PENELOPE

The PENELOPE was a light cruiser completed in 1936. During the war she was known as "The Shadow" and later, after she had been damaged in the Mediterranean, as the "Pepperpot". She had run aground during the Norwegian campaign in 1940, and was towed back to the UK, where repairs took until August 1941. She then became part of Force K in the Mediterranean operating against Italian convoys to North Africa. She took part in the Second Battle of Sirte and was intensively bombed in Malta, where she fired 75,000 rounds of ammunition in ten days. After repairs, she returned to the Mediterranean, and as this photograph shows, was fitted with tripod masts and her aircraft equipment replaced by pom poms. She became part of Force Q operating from North Africa and supported the landings at Salerno and Anzio. On 18 February 1944, whilst returning from the Anzio beaches, she was torpedoed by U410 and sank ten minutes later after a violent explosion.

75

PEVENSEY CASTLE

The PEVENSEY CASTLE was one of the 1060 ton Castle Class corvettes designed as a development of the Flower Class, and built by yards whose slips were too short to build the new frigates. She mounted a single 4 inch gun in A position, and a single squid anti-submarine mortar in B position. She had a single screw giving a speed of 16.5 knots. On 11 November 1944, she with three sisters, sank U1200 West of the Channel. Later she was with escort groups in the South West Approaches and later off the North of Scotland. In 1945 and 1946 she was employed on air sea rescue duties in the South Atlantic, before being placed in reserve from 1947 until 1952. In April 1960 she was refitted at Blyth and became the weather ship WEATHER MONITOR, later being renamed ADMIRAL BEAUFORT.

PIONEER

The PIONEER was a Colossus Class light fleet carrier that was completed by Vickers Armstrong at Barrow in January 1945, as a maintenance carrier. As can be seen from this photograph, she carried no aircraft, but there were workshops, cranes and guns fitted on her flight deck. She flew the broad pennant of the Commodore, Air Train, of the British Pacific Fleet in June 1945 and was at Manus when the Japanese surrender took place. She was placed in reserve at Rosyth in October 1946. She was recategorised as a ferry carrier in 1953, but was broken up at Inverkeithing in September 1954.

POLYANTHUS

The POLYANTHUS was a Flower Class corvette completed by Robb in April 1941. She was of an improved design, having a longer forecastle, foremast abaft the bridge and fitted with radar. The longer forecastle gave her more weight and made her slightly faster. She was used continuously on North Atlantic escort duties. In September 1943 she was part of the escort to a pair of convoys that were engaged by 19 U-boats over five days. Six merchant ships were lost together with three of their escorts, but three U boats were sunk and three others damaged. During that action she was hit by a homing torpedo from U952 and sank immediately. One survivor was rescued by the frigate ITCHEN, but the ITCHEN herself was torpedoed just two days later. There were only three survivors.

QUALITY

The destroyer QUALITY is photographed here in August 1942, just after commissioning at Swan Hunter. Armed with four single 4.7 inch guns in shields, and two quadruple torpedo tubes, this class were slightly longer than the earlier emergency war design destroyers and carried more AA guns. She was manned by the Royal Australian Navy during the war, and served in the East Indies from September 1943. In 1944 she was damaged by shore batteries at Sabang when she entered the harbour to attack with gunfire and torpedoes. In 1945 she was with the British Pacific Fleet and shelled Hitachi in July. She was transferred to the Royal Australian Navy at Melbourne on 25 October 1945 and later broken up, in Japan, in 1958.

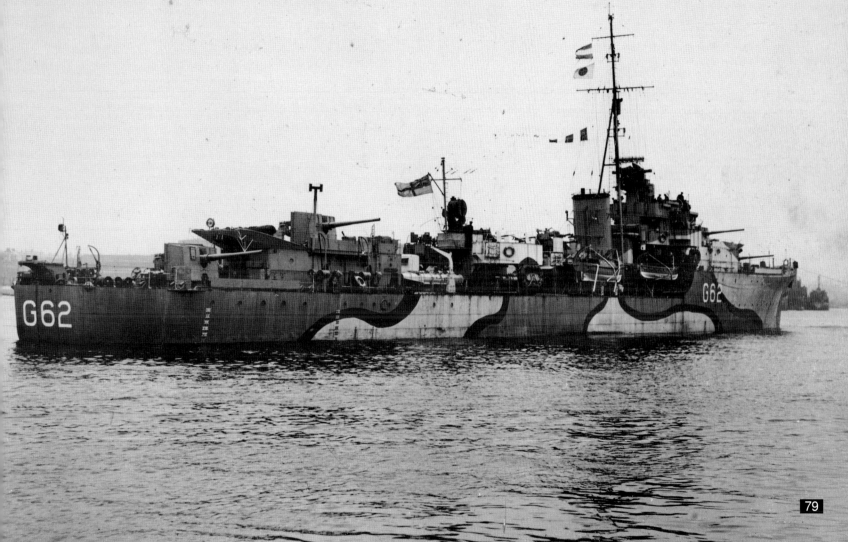

RAMILLIES

The battleship RAMILLIES is photographed in Plymouth Sound in 1943 with a Canadian Tribal Class destroyer visible beyond her quarterdeck. She and her sisters were never as dramatically modernised as the Queen Elizabeth Class battleships, and her original appearance was still discernable under a wealth of AA guns. She carried out a bombardment of Bardia in August 1940, but spent much of the early part of the war on convoy escort duties. She joined the Eastern Fleet and took part in the operation at Diego Suarez, being torpedoed by a Japanese midget submarine on 30 May 1942. She was repaired at Durban and Devonport. She rejoined the Eastern Fleet, but returned to the UK to provide fire support at the Normandy and South of France Landings before becoming part of the VERNON training establishment at Portsmouth. She was broken up in 1948.

H.M.S. RAMILLIES

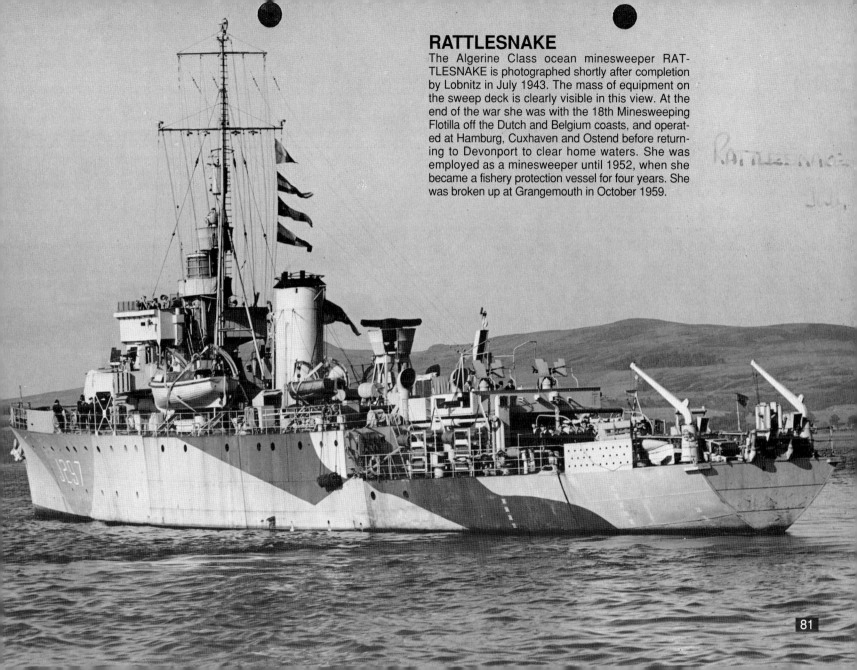

RATTLESNAKE

The Algerine Class ocean minesweeper RATTLESNAKE is photographed shortly after completion by Lobnitz in July 1943. The mass of equipment on the sweep deck is clearly visible in this view. At the end of the war she was with the 18th Minesweeping Flotilla off the Dutch and Belgium coasts, and operated at Hamburg, Cuxhaven and Ostend before returning to Devonport to clear home waters. She was employed as a minesweeper until 1952, when she became a fishery protection vessel for four years. She was broken up at Grangemouth in October 1959.

REPULSE

The battlecruiser REPULSE was completed in August 1916 and was in action in the Heligoland Bight in November 1917, when she hit the German cruiser KONIGS-BERG. Between the wars she did not receive the radical modernisation given to her sister ship RENOWN. She entered the war with an inadequate AA armament, which restricted her use. She was employed on convoy escort duty in the North Atlantic, and was with the Home Fleet during the Norwegian campaign in 1940. By February 1940 she had completed an exceptional 130 days at sea during the war. She was to receive little respite for the rest of her career. She was sent to Singapore to strengthen the fleet in the East, and was joined there by PRINCE OF WALES. REPULSE was recalled as she left for a visit to Australia. Both ships were sailed to investigate reports of Japanes landings in Malaya. Both were sunk by air attacks on 10 December 1941, 513 of the REPULSE's crew being lost.

REWARD

REWARD was a Bustler Class fleet tug launched at Leith on 13 October 1944. Powered by two Atlas Polar 8 cylinder diesels, her single screw could drive her 1100 tons at 16 knots. She was manned by the Royal Navy until 1952, and was then placed in reserve. In 1960-62 she was again Royal Navy manned and used for target towing off Malta. In 1960-65 she was on charter as the ENGLISHMAN. On return she became RFA manned until she was placed in reserve in 1973. Two years later she was refitted and became a patrol vessel for North Sea oilfields. On 10 August 1976 she collided with the German freighter PLAINSMAN in the Firth of Forth and sank. She was salvaged but was then broken up.

ROEBUCK

The destroyer ROEBUCK was "launched prematurely" by a near miss during an air raid at Greenock. This class were the last 'short' emergency war design destroyers, but differed from earlier vessels in that most officer accommodation was moved forward. Her radar, mounted on a mast between her torpedo tubes and surrounded by light AA guns looks ungainly in contrast with her otherwise sleek destroyer lines. She was completed in June 1943 and served in the East Indies, where she forced the U-boat tanker BRAKE to scuttle herself in March 1944. She also escorted carriers on raids on Sabang and took part in bombardments of Sabang, the Andaman Islands and Car Nicobar. In 1945 she supported amphibious landings in Burma and later operated off Malaya. She was converted to a fast anti-submarine frigate in 1951, used for explosive trials in 1968 and, later that year, broken up at Inverkeithing.

ROYAL SOVEREIGN

The ROYAL SOVEREIGN was launched at Portsmouth Dockyard in April 1915 and by 1939 had had few major modifications to her original design. She was employed on convoy escort work, a duty essential to deter surface raiders, and took part in the first engagement with the Italian Fleet off Calabria in July 1940. She joined the Eastern Fleet in 1942 and in 1943 returned to the UK for a refit, when four of her 6 inch guns were removed, as can be seen from this photograph taken at that time. After a period in Rosyth when she adopted the nom de plume HOPETOUN II, she was lent to the Russian Navy as the ARCHANGELSK - until February 1949. On her return she was broken up at Inverkeithing.

ROYALIST

The ROYALIST was a modified Dido Class cruiser, completed in August 1943, by Scotts at Greenock. This photograph was taken shortly afterwards. This class had a bridge one deck lower than the Didos, and mounted a pom pom in Q position instead of a fifth 5.25 inch turret. By reducing topweight, full radar control and power working could be fitted to the turrets and 2 pounder pom poms. Initially she served in the Arctic, and was then converted to an escort carrier squadron flagship with her torpedo tubes removed. She took part in the South of France landings. On 15 September 1944 she, and the destroyer TEAZER, sank two German ships in the Aegean. In May 1945 she took part in the capture of Rangoon. After the war she served as a training ship at Portsmouth, and was modernised at Devonport in 1954-56 before serving with the Royal New Zealand Navy. She was sold and broken up in Japan in 1968.

SAUCY

The SAUCY was a Flower Class corvette, launched by Harland and Wolff as the ARABIS in February 1940. Four months later she was in action in the North Atlantic against U122. In June 1941 she helped sink U651. She served with the 8th Escort Group, and Escort Group B8 until April 1942, when she was transferred to the US Navy and renamed SAUCY. She is photographed at that time wearing the US Naval Ensign. In that guise she continued escort duty in the Atlantic, but off the coast of Brazil. She was returned to the Royal Navy in 1945, and renamed SNAPDRAGON. She was sold into mercantile service (as the KATINA) in 1947.

SCEPTRE

The S Class submarine SCEPTRE was launched in January 1943 by Scotts and completed two months later. Of 715 tons and with a single 3 inch gun forward of her conning tower, she was fitted with seven torpedo tubes, and the after one of which is clearly visible in this photograph - taken in April 1943. She served in home waters during the war, not only on patrols off the Norwegian coast, but also towing midget submarines on attacks against the TIRPITZ and targets at Bergen. She was broken up at Gateshead in September 1949.

SCYLLA

The SCYLLA was a Dido Class cruiser launched by Scotts in June 1942. There was a shortage of 5.25 inch guns, and so she was fitted with four twin 4.5 inch guns instead. Shortly after completion she was part of the fighting escort provided for convoy PQ18 to Russia. She then went to the Mediterranean for the invasion of North Africa, and escorted ships along that coast. She returned to northern waters in December 1942, sinking the blockade runner RHAKOTIS on the way. She then escorted more Russian convoys, and took part in sweeps of the Bay of Biscay before returning to the Mediterranean for the Salerno landings. She had to return to the UK to have her engines repaired and became Admiral Vian's flagship at Normandy, where she was mined. She was never fully repaired and was broken up, in May 1950, at Barrow.

SHALIMAR

The SHALIMAR was launched by Chatham Dockyard on 22 April 1943 and is photographed among the Thames barges at the Nore in April 1944. She joined the Eastern Fleet on 28 September 1944, and was active on patrols in the Malacca Strait, sinking three coasters and over thirty small craft in patrols that lasted until July 1945. In November 1944, she bombarded targets on the Nicobar Islands. She visited Capetown prior to returning to the UK via Suez. She was laid up at Harwich on 30 October 1945, and arrived at Troon in July 1950, to be broken up.

SOKOL

The SOKOL was launched in September 1940, at Barrow as the U Class submarine URCHIN (P39). Of 540 tons, these submarines carried four torpedo tubes and a 3 inch gun. She was commissioned as the Polish SOKOL and joined the 9th Flotilla operating from Dundee, undertaking patrols in the Bay of Biscay. Later that year she joined the 10th Flotilla based on Malta, until she was damaged by near misses during air raids in March 1942. She was refitted at Blyth before returning to the Mediterranean in April 1943, and carried out patrols in the Aegean after the Italian surrender. She rejoined the 9th Flotilla at Dundee in 1944 after a refit. She then carried out patrols off Norway. She was returned to the Royal Navy in 1946 and was placed in reserve before being broken up at Gateshead in 1949.

STRONGBOW

The STRONGBOW was an S Class submarine launched by Scotts on 30 August 1943. She is photographed in January 1944 entering Larne harbour where there was a seaplane base. She served in the Eastern Fleet, arriving at Trincomalee on 10 August 1944 and undertook patrols in the Malacca Strait in 1944-45, sinking many small ships, junks and a tug. She also carried out unsuccessful attacks against two Japanese submarines, RO113 and RO115, in October 1944. She returned to the UK on 30 June 1945 and was laid up at Falmouth until being broken up at Preston in April 1946.

SUTTON

The SUTTON was a Later Hunt Class minesweeper launched in August 1918 at Dumbarton and remained in commission between the wars. She was coal burning and armed with a single 4 inch and 3 inch gun. At the outbreak of war she was in the Mediterranean, but returned to the UK in December 1939. She took part in the evacuation of Dunkirk, and is photographed here later in the war when fitted with an acoustic sweep on her bow. She took part in the Normandy Landings and was then placed in reserve at Falmouth on 22 December 1944. She was broken up in Belgium in 1947.

SWIFTSURE

The SWIFTSURE was in the third group of the Colony Class of cruisers, being completed on the Tyne in June 1944. She was built with only three triple 6 inch turrets, and not equipped to carry aircraft. Her AA armament was enhanced by an extra twin 4 inch gun in X position, clearly visible in this photograph taken shortly after her completion. She served in the British Pacific Fleet off Okinawa, and was with the force that re-occupied Hong Kong, the Japanese surrender being signed onboard. After the war she spent a period in reserve and then joined the Home Fleet. After a collision with the destroyer DIAMOND in 1953, she started a modernisation programme, but it was not completed and she was broken up in 1962.

TANTALUS

The TANTALUS was of the second group of the T Class submarines, fitted with three external stern torpedo tubes, clearly visible in this photograph taken in April 1943. She had been launched at Barrow two months earlier. She served with the 4th Flotilla in the Indian Ocean, sinking various ships and small craft as well as laying mines on patrols in the Malacca Strait. She also carried out air-sea rescue duties for the carrier strike on Sabang in July 1944 – and reconnaissance operations for the strike on Palembang in January 1945. She was broken up at Milford Haven in 1950.

TARTAR

The Tribal Class destroyer TARTAR is photographed in 1944, by which time she had been refitted with radar, a lattice foremast, a small mainmast, and a twin 4 inch gun in X position. She had been launched in October 1937, by Swan Hunter and took part in many of the major actions of the war, including the Norwegian campaign, the hunt for the BISMARCK, Operation Pedestal, Russian convoys and the landings in North Africa, Sicily and Normandy. She was one of the four Tribals to survive the war and was known as "Lucky Tartar". She took part in destroyer sweeps of the Channel in 1944, helping to sink several German destroyers and a convoy. She was placed in reserve in 1946 and was broken up at Newport in 1948.

H.M.S. "TARTAR"

TERMAGANT

The TERMAGANT was completed in December 1943 by Denny. In this class of emergency war design destroyers, the pom pom abaft the funnel had been removed, new gun shields introduced for the 4.7 inch guns and half the class were fitted with a short lattice foremast. She took part in Arctic convoys and then served in the Mediterranean, where she took part in the landings in the South of France and later helped sink two German torpedo boats in the Aegean. In 1945 she was with the British Pacific Fleet in Okinawa and in August shelled the island of Honshu. In 1952-53 she was given a limited conversion to become an anti-submarine frigate. She was broken up in 1965.

H.M.S. TORBAY

TORBAY

The TORBAY was in the first group of T Class submarines which were fitted with only one stern torpedo tube. She was launched in April 1940, at Chatham Dockyard and, early in 1941, helped guard Brest lest the German heavy units there tried to break out. She then went to the Mediterranean, where she sank the Italian submarine JANTINA off Izmir in July 1941, and attacked shipping in the Corfu Roads in March 1942, for which her Commanding Officer, Cdr. Miers, was awarded the Victoria Cross. She continued to serve in the Mediterranean, landing a force to attack Rommel's headquarters, and supporting the Sicilian landings. In 1945 she was employed on patrols in the Malacca Strait. She arrived at Briton Ferry for breaking up in January 1946.

TRACKER

The Ruler Class escort carrier TRACKER was commissioned in January 1943. She was of 11,420 tons, and had a full length hangar under her flight deck. She could carry 24 aircraft, and was armed with two 5 inch, sixteen 40mm and twenty 20mm guns. She was attached to escort groups in the North Atlantic on convoy protection duties, being with the Second Escort Group in 1943-44. Later in 1944 she escorted convoy JW58 to Russia. During this convoy her aircraft shared in the sinking of two U-boats. After helping protect the Normandy Landings against the U-boat threat, she escorted another convoy to Russia. She was returned to the US Navy in November 1945, becoming the mercantile CORRIENTES.

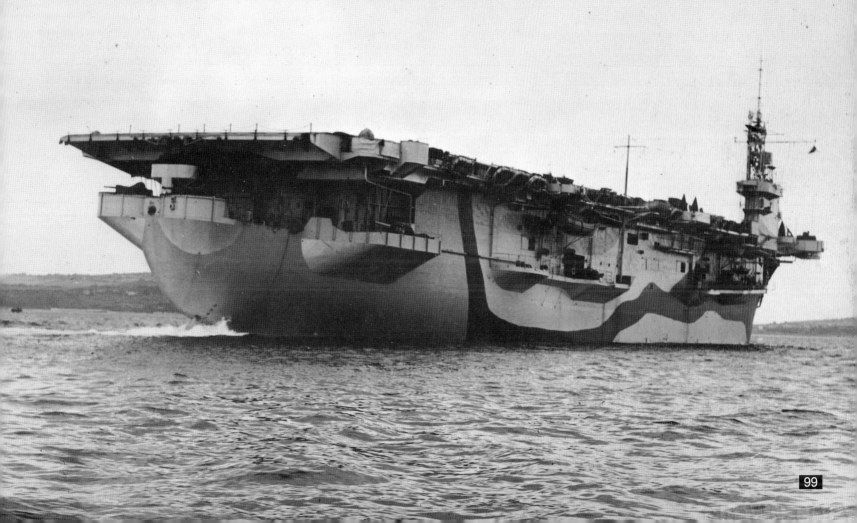

TRINIDAD

The Colony Class cruiser TRINIDAD was completed by Devonport Dockyard in October 1941. She is photographed shortly afterwards, with radar on her masts and directors. She was part of the escort to the Russian convoy PQ13 in March 1942. Three German destroyers sailed to intercept the convoy, and TRINIDAD and her escorting destroyers engaged them. TRINIDAD crippled the German Z26, but was then hit by one of her own torpedoes that she had fired at the German destroyer. She was taken to Murmansk for temporary repairs, and sailed on 13 May for the UK with a destroyer escort. She was attacked by torpedo aircraft and dive bombers, and, towards the end of the action, received a hit which started fires, whilst a near miss damaged the temporary repairs carried out at Murmansk. Manoeuvres to avoid further attacks fanned the fires onboard, and she had to be abandoned. She was sunk by the destroyer MATCHLESS on 15 May 1942.

TYNWALD
Originally built as a twin screw passenger ship, TYNWALD took part in the evacuation of Dunkirk, rescuing nearly 10,000 soldiers. She was requisitioned in July 1940, and converted to an auxiliary anti-aircraft ship. She had steam turbines giving her a speed of 21 knots. After conversion, she mounted three twin 4 inch guns and two quadruple pom poms. She served on escort duty in the Irish Sea. She escorted convoys to Gibraltar for the North African landings, and then operated along that coast. On 12 November 1942 she ran into a mine laid by the Italian submarine ARGO in Bougie harbour and sank rapidly.

UGANDA

The UGANDA was of the second group of the Colony Class of cruisers, having a squarer bridge and sacrificing X turret for a heavier AA armament. She was completed on the Tyne in December 1942, and served in the Mediterranean at the landings at Sicily and Salerno. She was badly damaged at the latter in September 1943. After repairs in the USA, she was presented to the Royal Canadian Navy in October 1944, and served with the British Pacific Fleet in 1945 during attacks on the Sakishima-Gunto group of islands and the Japanese homeland. She became a training cruiser after the war, and renamed QUEBEC in April 1951. She was broken up at Osaka in 1961.

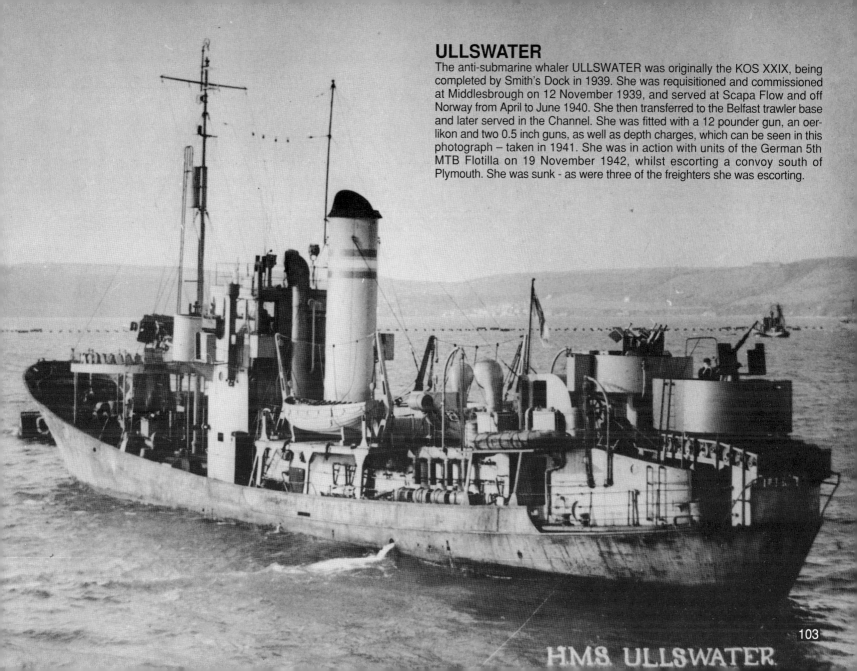

ULLSWATER

The anti-submarine whaler ULLSWATER was originally the KOS XXIX, being completed by Smith's Dock in 1939. She was requisitioned and commissioned at Middlesbrough on 12 November 1939, and served at Scapa Flow and off Norway from April to June 1940. She then transferred to the Belfast trawler base and later served in the Channel. She was fitted with a 12 pounder gun, an oerlikon and two 0.5 inch guns, as well as depth charges, which can be seen in this photograph – taken in 1941. She was in action with units of the German 5th MTB Flotilla on 19 November 1942, whilst escorting a convoy south of Plymouth. She was sunk - as were three of the freighters she was escorting.

HMS ULLSWATER

VALIANT

The battleship VALIANT had been completed in 1916, and was present at
Jutland. Between the wars she was radically modernised, and served in
the Mediterranean in 1941 - at Matapan and Crete. She was damaged at
Crete, and again in December 1941, during an Italian attack on Alexandria.
After a period in the Eastern Fleet, she returned to the Mediterranean for
the Sicilian and Salerno landings. She escorted the Italian Fleet to its surrender. She is photographed in 1943, and her enhanced AA armament
can be seen in this view. Late in 1943 she joined the Eastern Fleet and
took part in bombardments, but was damaged when a floating dock she
was in at Trincomalee collapsed. She had to return to the UK via the Cape
and became a training ship at Devonport before being sold in 1948.

VISCOUNT

One of two Thornycroft V Class destroyers, the VISCOUNT had been launched in 1917, and had an extra 3,000 shaft horse power to give her an extra knot in speed. In May 1941 she was damaged during an air raid on Liverpool. She was converted to a long range escort, with her forward boiler removed to allow her extra fuel stowage. Her A gun was replaced by a hedgehog anti-submarine mortar and Y gun removed to make more room for depth charges. She was employed escorting North Atlantic convoys and, in October 1942, detected U661 by radar and rammed her at 26 knots. In February 1943 she sank U201, again by ramming. She was sold in March 1945 for breaking up.

H.M.S. "VISCOUNT"
1942

WATCHMAN

The WATCHMAN had been launched in December 1917, and was employed on fleet duties in the Mediterranean in 1940, and later on North Atlantic escort duties. In 1943, she was converted to a long range escort, with her forward boiler removed and gunnery armament reduced, but with extra depth charge throwers and charges, and with a hedgehog mortar in A position. Her minelaying stern can still be seen in this photograph. She was in the Channel for the Normandy Landings and attacked E boats (suspected of minelaying) in Lyme Bay. On 6 April 1945 she sank U1195 twelve miles South East of Sandown. She paid off in July 1945, and was taken to Inverkeithing that month for breaking up.

WEAR

The frigate WEAR is photographed just after completion in October 1942, by Smith's Dock. Some of this class were fitted for minelaying, and such equipment can be seen on her quaterdeck abaft the depth charge throwers and rails. She served in the North Atlantic and on patrols in the Bay of Biscay. She paid off in August 1946 and was placed in reserve at Harwich and later at West Hartlepool, where she was the headquarters ship of the local reserve fleet from 1954-55. She was broken up at Sunderland in October 1957.

WESTLYN

The trawler WESTLYN was requisitioned in 1940, and was employed on boom defence duties at Devonport. She is photographed in 1943 off Drake's Island standing by the booms in Plymouth Sound. She had been launched in 1914 and was of 284 tons. She was sold in May 1947.

H.M.B.D.V. WESTLYN.
1943.

WOLSEY

The WOLSEY had been built in 1918 as a fleet destroyer, and on trials achieved 38.2 knots, the fastest of all V & W destroyers. In December 1939, she was converted to an escort vessel. She was then armed with twin 4 inch guns in A and X position and fitted with a new bridge. She took part in the Dunkirk evacuation in May 1940, where although damaged, recovered over 3,300 troops. Later she defended coastal convoys against E boat attacks. She is photographed (with radar mounted amidships) in October 1944 in the Firth of Forth. On 14 May 1945 she and the WOLFHOUND entered Stavanger to take the German surrender there. She was broken up at Sunderland in March 1947.

WOLVERINE

The WOLVERINE had been launched by White in July 1919 and was originally armed with four 4.7 inch guns and six torpedo tubes. In May 1940 she assisted with the Norwegian campaign, and the next month helped evacuate St Nazaire. In March 1941 she sank U47 and, a month later, U76 in the North Atlantic. She was converted to a short range escort, retaining her original propulsion machinery, but reducing her gunnery armament in favour of more anti-submarine weapons. In August 1942, whilst escorting the carrier FURI-OUS in the Mediterranean, she sank the Italian submarine DAGABUR by ramming. She was placed in reserve in June 1945, and sold in January 1946.

H.M.S. WOLVERINE.

ZENITH

ZENITH, originally to have been called WESSEX, was completed in December 1944, by Denny. The Z Class of emergency war design destroyers were the first class fitted with 4.5 inch guns, and they had a single large director (Mk 1 Type K) on the bridge. There had been a steady development in the emergency war classes, and ZENITH showed the removal of the searchlight aft of the funnel. extra light AA guns, as well as catwalks over the torpedo tubes. This class were "arcticised" and served on Russian convoys. ZENITH remained with the Home Fleet until put in reserve in 1947. She was sold to Egypt in 1955 and renamed EL FATEH.

INDEX